Time Zones

Thrillogy

Edited by Paul Collins and Meredith Costain

sundance

Read all of the

 Titles

Fantasy/Horror

Dragon Tales

Ghosts and Ghoulies

Heroic Feats

Last Gasps

Tales from Beyond

Terrors of Nature

Science Fiction

Alien Invasions

Gadgets and Gizmos

It Came from the Lab . . .

Lost in Space

Techno Terror

Time Zones

Published by Sundance Publishing
P.O. Box 1326, 234 Taylor Street, Littleton, MA 01460

First published 1999 as Spinouts by
Addison Wesley Longman Australia Pty Limited
95 Coventry Street, South Melbourne 3205 Australia
Exclusive United States Distribution: Sundance Publishing

ISBN 0-7608-4826-2

Printed in Canada

Contents

Time Out

The author
Damien Broderick
talks about the story

"Time travel is my favorite science fiction idea. I was quite young when I first realized you could leave a message for time travelers to come and visit, and I've since heard of other people with the same idea. No visits yet — as far as I know. I don't think I've had any, either. But it might have slipped my mind."

Time Out

My best friend, Tiger Thieu, had an awesome birthday party last Sunday. He got a new bike, computer games, some money, and the weirdest present I've ever heard of.

His Uncle Po bought him a twenty-five-word message to be included in the time capsule that'll be placed in a vault in the new library. Tiger could write any message he wanted on a card, and in 200 years people would read it. Tiger politely thanked his uncle, but you could tell he'd been hoping for something better.

After Tiger opened his presents, we played laser tag outside, and the party got pretty noisy. I noticed that the grouchy old lady from next door was peering over the fence. I grabbed Tiger as he ran past.

"Hey, Tiges, the old crow is going to call the cops on us."

He had whipped cream all over his face.
"Mmnfle?"

"Look, she's trying to hide behind that rosebush."

Her beady little eyes glinted. I watched her reach out with one hand to push the roses aside to get a better view and heard her give a muffled cry and snatch her hand back. I almost fell over laughing.

"Ha ha! Stuck herself on the thorns! What a pain she is."

All of us kids grabbed doughnuts and soda and went down to the end of the yard. We crowded into Tiger's clubhouse.

"What'll we play now?" asked Kostas, who never has any good ideas for games. He's big, though, very useful if some bully comes up and tries to push you around.

"Let's pretend this is the *Millennium Falcon*," Tiger told him. He sat on a wooden box and turned on the old computer we'd found in the local dump. There was no keyboard, and it didn't do much. But the screen saver looked like you were sitting inside a spaceship, plunging into the middle of millions of stars.

"Boring," I said.

"Yeah, well *you* think of something," said Melanie Estabrook. "If you're so smart."

"Who let a *girl* in here?" Kostas yelled in outrage, but Melanie just stared him in the eye until he sat down. Melanie wasn't as big as Kostas, but she never backed down and could make your life miserable if you got in her way. It looked, for a moment, as if there was going to be a brawl, but then I had my great idea.

"Let's make a time machine!" I yelped.

"Aw, yeah," Tiger said, with an interested expression. "Hmm. We could pretend to go into

9

the future and check out all of the new inventions."

"No, listen!" I shouted, spraying Zipper Finucane with spit. "A *real* time machine!"

"Aw, get real, peanut-brain," Melanie said. "There's no such thing."

"Not yet," I admitted. "But there will be someday."

Tiger looked at me, mouth gaping. "They'll have time machines in the future," he said. That kid's smart.

"And they'll come back in them, because our time is the past to them!" I added. "I know what we can do that will almost be like having a time machine! We could trap a time traveler."

They all looked at me. I flabbergasted them. I gulped, afraid that I'd made a complete idiot of myself.

"How are you going to do *that*?" Melanie asked.

"We could send them a message," I said.

Tiger Thieu reached into his jacket pocket. He took out the envelope his Uncle Po had given him.

"We could invite them to come back and visit us," he said.

"Yep," I said. "Now we need to find the right way to say it, so they'll really want to come."

There was an incredible racket. Everyone in the

clubhouse yelled and pushed and wanted it explained. I told them the mayor was going to put a whole bunch of stuff — like newspapers, clothes, and toys from the end of the twentieth century — inside this time capsule. In 200 years, people would open the vault and find the time capsule. They'd read Tiger's message, and if there were time machines by then, they'd come back and visit us.

"We'll tell them to aim for today." I looked at my watch. It was 6:15. I burped and said, "We'd better write down 6:30. That's in fifteen minutes. We'll tell them the address and ask them to land their ship in the yard."

"Mrs. Gladstone will freak!" Tiger said.

"Yeah, worse than getting stabbed by rosebush thorns."

We practiced writing our message on a scrap of paper. Melanie said the spelling was wrong, so we fixed it, and I printed it pretty neatly on Tiger Thieu's card. He put the envelope back in his pocket.

"Now what?" said Kostas. He stuck his head out the clubhouse door. "There's no time machine here."

"Of course not, it's only 6:27."

"But how could they know about it already? We didn't send it," Sanders said.

"Doesn't matter," Tiger told him. "Uncle Po will mail it, and it will go into the time capsule, and in 200 years someone will open it and then come back here." He frowned. "I think."

At 6:30 there was a sound outside. The door of the clubhouse opened.

Mrs. Gladstone, the busybody from next door, stuck her big head around the corner.

Kostas screamed and fainted. Melanie whacked Zipper in the eye by mistake. Tiger stood up from his old computer and stepped forward.

"*You* are from the future?"

Mrs. Gladstone came in. "Of course," she said.

"But you weren't supposed to get here until now," I said. "You've been living next door to the Thieus ever since they moved here!" Spying on them, I thought.

Oh, now I got it. She had come back sooner than we'd said to, so that she could check out who these

people were who'd invited the time travelers back to visit.

"Correct," she told me, looking deep into my eyes. I hadn't said a word. Could she . . .

"Yes, I can read your mind, young man, with the help of a little machine. In my time, we have machines to do just about everything." She shook her head sadly. "Everything except think up new ideas."

"I thought you'd have intelligent machines," I said, my voice trembling.

"Oh, we do," said the woman who called herself Mrs. Gladstone. "They have figured out how to travel in time. But they can only invent things based on our ideas, and we've become so reliant on machines, we've lost our imaginations. So I was sent here to look for people who have imagination."

I shrank back against the bench where the old PC was still showing stars pouring through the depths of space. But Tiger wasn't scared. His eyes gleamed.

"Do they have spaceships in your time?" he asked.

"Oh yes, you can travel to any planet you want. Few of us do any longer. But you can certainly take the grand tour, Tiger, if you choose to come back with me." She glanced at me. "You can come too."

"I — I — I" was about to wet myself. Just leave everything behind? My family and all my pals, like dumb old Kostas, who was groaning and waking up. "Not me, Mrs. Gladstone. I'm staying here."

She sighed, a little disappointed. "Very well. So, Tiger? We'll make sure your parents know that you are in good hands. They will be upset, of course, but we will find ways to make them understand."

My skin crawled. Maybe their machines could also wipe out memories. But Tiger Thieu was shivering with excitement.

He took the envelope out of his pocket and handed it to me.

"Mail this tomorrow, will you, buddy?"

"I'll even put a stamp on it," I said. I punched him on the shoulder, and he and Mrs. Gladstone pushed past us. The clubhouse door closed behind them, and there was a popping sound.

When we rushed out, they were nowhere to be seen. Of course, I knew where they were. They were in the year 2200 and my pal Tiger Thieu was sailing the depths of space in a starship.

Then the creepiest thing of all happened. All of the other kids just sort of wandered away, with a funny blank look in their eyes. Dr. Thieu and his family watched us all leave the party without a word, as if they didn't see us. I went home and had dinner, and

couldn't think of any way to tell my parents about what had happened.

After dinner, I asked Mom for a postage stamp.

Then I walked to the mailbox on the corner. I stood there a while, thinking about what would

happen if I didn't mail Tiger's message. Maybe everything would go back to the way it had been before. But then I thought about how excited Tiger had been about riding in a spaceship. So I opened the mailbox and dropped the letter in.

The next day I tried to tell my mother everything.

"You know my best friend, Tiger Thieu?" I said.

My mother shook her head, sorting socks as she took them out of the dryer.

"I don't think so, honey. Which one is he?"

Tiger had dinner at our place just the week before. I felt cold, and sick, and said nothing.

I hope he'll come back some day. I'd like to hear about the world of the future, all of those starships and smart machines.

But I'm afraid that by then I'll have forgotten all about him, too.

Virtual Homecoming

The author
Beverley MacDonald
talks about the story

"Science fiction introduced me to the slippery nature of time. Time is not like a universal clock but is relative to how fast you are traveling. Spaceships must travel very fast to cross the enormous distances between the stars. What would it be like to live in such a world, to live in the future?"

Virtual Homecoming

Zoe read the last question again. *What year was the first starship commissioned?* Zoe couldn't remember. Was it 2053 or 2052? Zoe hated school tests, but she couldn't leave until she was finished. So she chose 2052 and uploaded her answers. There was a fifty percent chance she was right.

It didn't take long.

Miss Azulai's frowning face appeared on the screen.

"Zoe. Didn't you study for this test?"

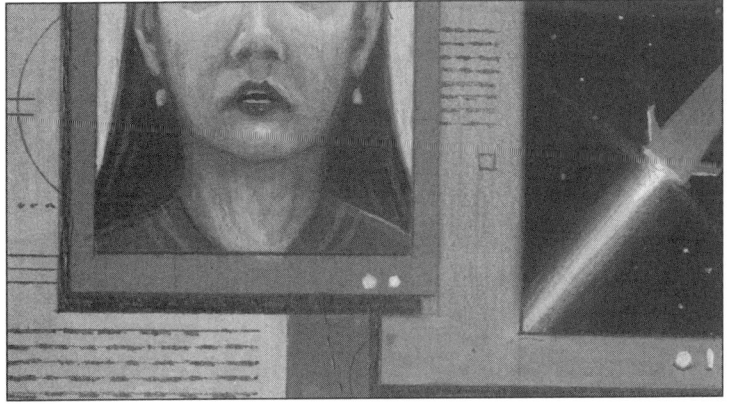

"Um." Zoe squirmed. Actually, she hadn't studied, but she had hoped she'd slide that past her teaching supervisor. "Sorry. It's just that my grandmother comes home today. And I've been busy," Zoe finished lamely. Now she was in for it. Miss Azulai was very strict and never accepted any excuse — not even a broken arm. When her classmate, Billy, broke his arm, Miss Azulai just told him to use his other one.

"Zoe, if you want to follow in your grandmother's footsteps, you'll have to work a lot harder." Miss Azulai scowled. She knew about Zoe's grandmother. She was famous, very famous.

"Oh, I do. I mean, I will," Zoe mumbled. She wanted nothing more than to be a starship pilot, just like her grandmother, the first woman astronavigator. Oh, Zoe knew her parents didn't approve. Every time Zoe brought up the subject, her father frowned and told her not to be silly. Her mother just got quiet. Grandma had been away for a long time, and Zoe eventually realized that her mother missed her grandmother. She soon learned not to ask so many questions.

But at night, Zoe would sneak out into the back yard and lie on the astrolawn. She would look up at the stars and wonder what her grandmother was doing at that moment. Was she meeting aliens? No

one had met aliens so far, but the scientists said they must be out there.

Was she asleep or having lunch? What would she be eating? Occasionally, Zoe would be lucky enough to glimpse a sparkling trail of light streaking upward into the night sky. It was another shuttle taking passengers up to the great starships that orbited beyond the moon. Zoe pretended she was on board, preparing for her first flight — the greatest adventure of all!

"Zoe?" Miss Azulai wasn't finished yet. "For homework, write one hundred words on the relationship between time and space. Remember that time slows down the faster you travel."

"I promise," Zoe hastily agreed. Her hand hovered above the keyboard.

"Not so fast, Zoe. I'll expect your essay tomorrow." Miss Azulai smiled, and from halfway across the world her face faded from the screen.

"Hi, Zoe." Billy's grin appeared.

"How's the arm?" Zoe liked Billy, though she'd never met him in person. Billy lived in South Africa. Zoe's class, which was scattered across the world, had been selected for compatibility by computer, matched with a teaching supervisor, and linked by electronic webs to their virtual classroom. In her most wicked thoughts, Zoe

considered that even Miss Azulai might not be real, nothing more than a clever program — a virtual teacher.

"It's better." Billy held up his arm so Zoe could see. "But don't tell Miss Azulai. I'm still working on her sympathy."

Zoe laughed. "Good luck." She figured he'd need it. "See ya tomorrow, Billy."

"See ya, Zoe."

Zoe cleared the screen and pushed her chair away from the console. So much for school.

"Finished already?" It was Zoe's dad.

"Dad! You're not supposed to eavesdrop on my lessons! Don't I have any privacy around here?"

Her father's eyebrows rose. "I could help you with your homework, if you want."

"I thought you didn't want me to be an astronavigator?" Zoe was astonished.

"That's not what I mean. But remember, your grandmother has been away for a long time. Here, you can give me a hand." Her father lifted the banner he was carrying. "What do you think?" he asked Zoe. "I thought I'd hang it over the front door."

"I'm sure she'll love it." Zoe helped her father put up the banner outside. "Did you ever meet Grandma?" Zoe asked, admiring their work.

"Welcome Home," in bright red letters was draped across the front porch.

Her father shook his head. "Your mother was just a baby when she left. Why don't you clean up your room, or play with the dog, or something?"

Zoe's eyebrows rose. She'd put the dog in a closet months ago when she'd decided she was too old for virtual pets. No, this wasn't about the dog. Her father wanted some privacy. Well, that was fine with Zoe.

"Sure." Zoe shrugged and wandered back inside. It took a while to find the dog, and when a pile of junk tumbled from the top shelf onto her head, Zoe decided she should clean up her room — soon, but not just now.

"Aha!" Zoe hauled the white fur from the back of the shelf. The little dog was deactivated, and Zoe plugged it into a socket to recharge. It would take a few minutes. While she waited, she worked on shoving the mess back into her closet. But when a stack of cubes tumbled to the floor, Zoe stopped and picked one up, turning it over in her hand.

The movement activated the hologram, and the image of a beautiful young woman dressed in an astronavigator's uniform smiled out at Zoe. It was Zoe's grandmother, photographed while accepting her first starship commission. If Zoe turned out to

be half as beautiful, or half as smart, she'd be happy.

The dog barked, announcing it was now recharged and ready to play. "Hold on," smiled Zoe, unplugging the dog.

It shook its white fur and rolled over, furiously wagging its tail. It looked up at Zoe and barked. The dog was really cute — for a toy. But nobody owned real dogs any more. They were too dirty, too much trouble, too expensive to feed. Virtual dogs never needed to be walked, or fed, or cleaned up after. You could put them in a closet for months, and they still loved you when you took them out. It made Zoe very sad. She deactivated the little dog and placed it back in the closet. She was too old for toys.

"Zoe!" It was her mother calling. Her worried frown changed to a smile as she entered the bedroom. "I don't believe it. You're cleaning your room."

"Hi, Mom." Zoe kissed her mother. "You're home early."

Before her mother could answer, the phone rang, and the front doorbell chimed.

Zoe's mother fished in her pocket, activated her phone, and waved to Zoe to answer the door. But

her father got there first. Zoe stared at the beautiful woman framed in the doorway. There was something familiar about her.

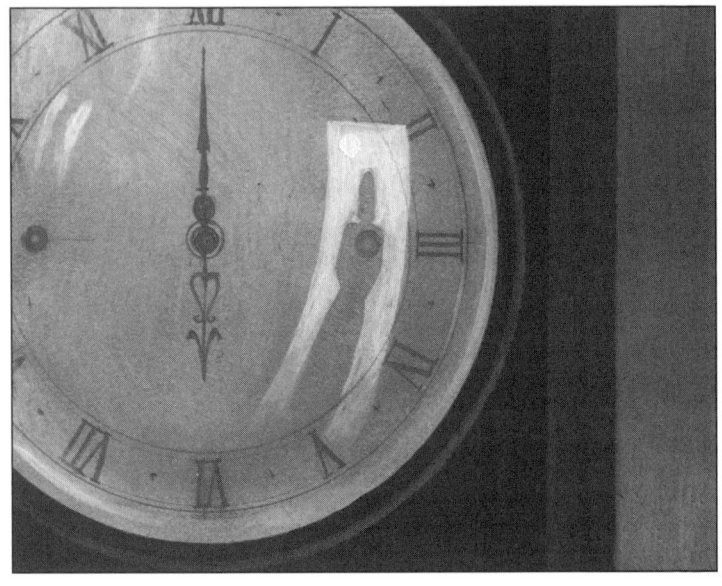

"You must be Helen?" She smiled at Zoe.

Zoe was confused. This was the same woman she'd seen in the holocube. She was exactly the same.

"No." Her father shook his head. "This is Zoe. Your granddaughter."

Zoe's mother walked into the room, phone still in hand. "They called to say she'll be early . . ."

She trailed off, staring at the beautiful stranger. "Mom?"

There was a long, long silence.

It took Zoe a while to understand. They were eating dinner before everything fell into place. It was the relationship between time and space. She'd never really understood what that meant before — how the faster a starship traveled, the more time slowed down for people on board. For Zoe's grandmother, traveling at almost the speed of light, only a few months had passed since she had kissed her baby daughter good-bye and climbed aboard the starship. But nearly forty years had passed for the people she'd left behind on Earth.

Zoe stared at the two women, trying to figure it out. It made her brain hurt to think about the slippery nature of time. Her grandmother was younger than her mother. In fact, her grandmother wasn't much older than Zoe!

Later, Zoe slipped away from the dinner table and wandered into the backyard. It was nearly dark, and she sat down on the astrolawn, hugging her knees. Nobody had real lawns any more. Virtual lawns never needed to be watered, or mowed, or anything. Real things were too much trouble. Zoe watched the first stars glitter overhead in the

evening light. At least they weren't virtual. Something in the world was still real.

"Star light, star bright, first star I see tonight." A voice said, "I wish I may, I wish I might, have this wish I wish tonight." It was Zoe's grandmother. "Are you wishing on stars, Zoe?"

"It's not a star, Grandma. It's Venus. Sorry, but it feels weird calling you Grandma."

"It feels weird for me, too," smiled her grandmother, sitting down beside her. "But I'm glad you can tell the difference between a planet and a star. Do you want to be an astronavigator, Zoe?"

"Are you going away again?" Zoe asked, changing the subject.

Her grandmother nodded. "I'm only here for a month."

"Is that why Mom and Dad don't want me to be an astronavigator?"

"Well, it's something to think about. The next time I come home . . ."

". . . Mom and Dad might have grown old and died," Zoe finished.

"That's true, Zoe. We all have to live with our choices. It's your life, and nobody can make those decisions for you."

"No," Zoe whispered, looking back to the sky. For the briefest moment a sparkling trail of light flashed upward — a shuttle, arcing through space. Zoe closed her eyes and wished.

Grandma

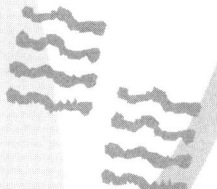

The author
Jackie French
talks about the story

"I've always been fascinated by time. The more you think about it, the weirder it gets!"

Grandma

The doorbell rang a third time.

"Mom!"

No answer.

"Mom! Someone's at the door!"

Still no answer. Maybe Mom was still in the shower and hadn't heard it. Robert yelled louder.

"Mom, I'm busy. Someone's at the door!"

The doorbell rang again. This time Robert went to answer it, holding his magazine carefully, so he wouldn't lose his place. He was reading a great article about "ripples" in space-time. He was crazy about space, gravity, physics, and especially, time travel.

Robert opened the door and blinked at the sunlight.

A small boy stood on the doormat, clutching a red bag with strange cartoon characters on it. His hair was brown, his eyes green and wide and sort of scared-looking. He looked familiar.

"Can I help you?" Robert said.

"I'm looking for Grandma."

"Excuse me?"

"Grandma. I'm looking for her." The boy blinked at Robert with frightened eyes.

Robert closed his magazine over his thumb, to keep his place.

"Sorry, I think you have the wrong house."

The boy shook his head. "No, this is it. This is my grandma's house. Dad said I should come here fast."

"Look, kid, this can't be your grandma's. There's just Mom and me living here. No one else." Robert started to close the door.

"Robert, who is it?" His mother came out of the bathroom, drying her hair. "Who's at the door?"

"Grandma!" The child's face lit up. He rushed through the door and down the hall and grabbed her around the knees. Suddenly, he was sobbing. "The boy wouldn't let me in, and I *know* you're my grandma. Daddy said I should come to you right now! He said they're coming *now*. That's why he sent me through the fuzzy waves."

Robert stared as his mother's arms closed automatically around the child. "Honey, I don't understand."

The child stood back for a moment. "Grandma, your . . . your hair is different," he said, puzzled. "I've never seen that dress before. Grandma, you won't let them take me away, will you? You'll keep me safe until Daddy gets here."

"Sure, you're safe here. Isn't he, Robert?"

"Mom!"

His mother gave him a warning look. "We've got to figure this out somehow, Robert. Would you mind . . ."

"Look Mom, I'm right in the middle of this article about time travel. It could be possible in the near future."

"For Pete's sake, Robert!" The child was still sobbing. "Go and finish your article, then. Just try to remember to set the table — for three, I guess."

Robert watched her lift the child into her arms and open the living room door. He felt as though he should do something, as though he should help in some way. But his mom would handle it. She always did.

The living room was next to his bedroom. No matter how he tried to concentrate, voices floated through.

"And Daddy said that if they came, I should come to you . . . there might not be much time . . ."

"Who would come, honey? Just slow down."

". . . the Cold Ones are coming . . . I thought they'd get me, I could feel their cold. You can feel it all through you, Grandma. Daddy will tell you. He said that he'd get here tonight, that he'd go into the fuzzy waves too, and that would bring him here, where the Cold Ones can't find us."

"What fuzzy waves?"

"You know, Grandma, the fuzzy waves. Daddy says they're our best weapon yet, and . . ."

Kids! This one had been watching too much science fiction on TV, thought Robert. On the other hand, those fuzzy waves sounded a lot like the ripples in time he was reading about . . .

Robert put the magazine down and went out to the kitchen. The kid was watching television, some old rerun, but he seemed to like it. Robert had stopped watching kids' shows years ago.

His mother came into the kitchen while he was setting the table. "Is he staying for dinner?" Robert asked her.

"He might have to stay for a while."

"Why?"

"Because he doesn't have anywhere else to go. And he seems so sure that he knows me."

"Hey, Mom." Robert suddenly remembered something. "Miss Cranshaw at school told me about this new book that just came out. It's all about dark matter. She's not going to order it for the library, 'cause she says I'm the only kid who'd read it. So I wondered if you could get it for me?"

"Robert, I was trying to tell you something about this boy. Do you mind if he stays here for a while?"

"Mind?" Robert considered. "No. I guess not. But what about his parents? They'll be looking for him."

His mother looked at him strangely. "Do you want to help me look for them?"

"No," said Robert hurriedly. "I've got stuff I want to look at after dinner."

"The boy says his father knows he's here. I think it's best if he stays," said Robert's mother.

"You handle it, Mom. It's fine with me. You won't forget about the book, will you? I have the name written down somewhere."

"I won't forget," said his mother.

"What's for dinner?"

"Lasagna," she said, and opened the oven.

The kid's table manners were awful. He ate the cheese topping with his fingers.

"Try using your fork, honey," said Robert's mother.

"That's what it's there for."

"Aw, Grandma!" said the kid. "You're always saying that."

"Just use your fork." She sounded worried, but she was smiling. She gently reached over and showed the kid how to hold the fork.

"What's your name?" Robert asked suddenly.

The kid looked up at him. "Stephen."

Like the physicist Stephen Hawking, thought Robert. It was a good name to give a kid. Hawking's *A Brief History of Time* was one of his favorite books, although he didn't agree with Hawking about everything. Robert turned back to his lasagna. If he hurried, he might get that other article read tonight, before he started his homework. Then, there was that article Mrs. Harris, his science teacher, had given him.

"Robert?"

Robert looked up.

"I said, do you want any dessert?"

"Yeah, sure Mom."

His mother dished out peaches and ice cream. Stephen began spooning them up like there was no tomorrow, chattering away at the same time. Robert started thinking about something he'd read

in the Stephen Hawking book — that real time might just be part of our imagination. That imaginary time has no limits and no boundaries . . .

Robert stood up, his mind still on the book, and began to clear the table.

"I'll do the dishes," his mother said.

"Gee, thanks Mom. Mrs. Harris gave me this article, and I just got this new idea. I need to think it through."

"Run along," said his mother. "Stephen will help me. Won't you?"

"Sure landings!" said Stephen.

He was a funny kid. He seemed happier now, like he was right at home, like he'd always been here. *Always.* What was always? Until the end of the universe? Until time broke down? There were so many questions!

The doorbell rang just as he read the final page. He wondered if he should answer it, or maybe just keep Mom company, if it was more trouble.

Robert could hear Mom's footsteps in the hall. He listened to her open the door. He could hear voices — Mom's and someone else's. It was a man's voice. Stephen's father, probably.

Then Mom sounded different, almost as if she was scared. Robert put down the magazine and opened his bedroom door.

His mother stood in the hall. She was talking to a stranger. He was dressed in jeans and a shirt, but there was something unusual about them.

He overheard the man say, ". . . I knew you would take care of him."

His mother seemed to be confused, and he thought he heard her call the stranger "Robert." That would be funny, if Stephen's dad had the same name as he did.

The man looked at him. He had green eyes just like Stephen. Sort of familiar eyes, thought Robert. Maybe he'd seen them in a photo once.

"Hello, Robert!" said the stranger. He grinned a funny grin. "You look just like I remember."

Robert shrugged. He waited for the man to give his name, but he didn't.

Robert glanced at his mother. She looked amazed.

"Robert. Well, my sinking stars," said the man. He was still grinning, a really weird grin, like he was seeing something that he'd never expected to see. There were lines of worry around his eyes. "Who would have thought it?"

Robert frowned at his mother. Why didn't she introduce the man to him? She shook her head. "It's fine, Robert," she said. "I'll explain later, honey. You go back to your reading."

"I finished it."

"Well, go do your homework, then."

Robert hesitated, but she seemed all right. "You sure you're okay? I just have another chapter to read." He turned back to his room.

"You're reading Hawking!" said the man suddenly.

Robert turned slowly. "How'd you know that?"

"I guessed," said the man.

"Have you read him?" asked Robert eagerly.

"Yes, when I was about your age."

45

"But you couldn't have. It was only written in . . ."

Robert tried to figure out when the book had been published — it wasn't that long ago — but he gave up. "What did you think of it? What about that stuff he says about imaginary time?"

"I didn't agree with Hawking, either," said the man. His smile was peculiar, and his eyes were sad.

Suddenly Stephen came racing down the hall.

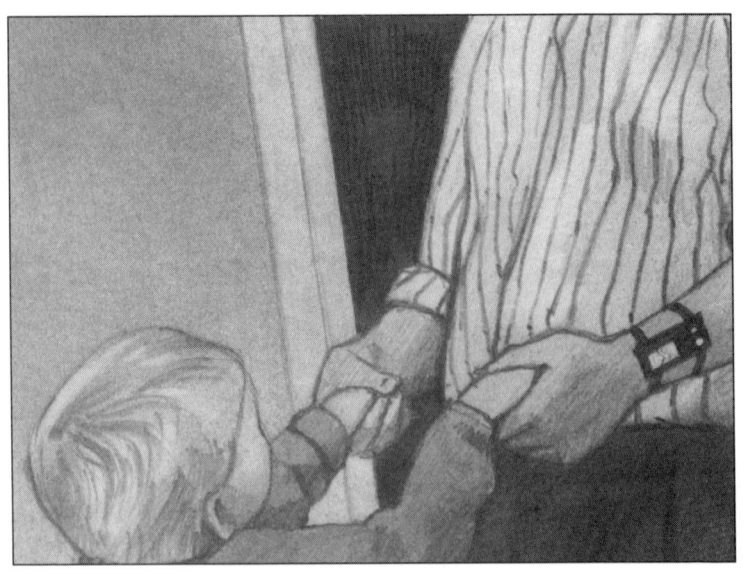

"Daddy!" he shrieked. The man picked him up. "Daddy, you're safe!"

"I sure am," said the man. "But more importantly, so are you."

"Can you stay?"

"Only for a few minutes," said the man. "That's all I can manage this time. The harnessing is still partially incomplete. But I'll be back. You'll be safe here." He looked at Robert's mother. "He *can* stay here, can't he?"

"Of course," she said. "Of course he can. Always. As long as you need him to stay."

Watching the stranger with Stephen, Robert got a funny feeling. It almost felt like deja vu, like it was something he'd seen or experienced before.

Robert went back to his bedroom. He had a lot to think about. How did the stranger know he was reading Hawking's book? It was interesting that he agreed with Robert about Hawking's theories about time. Why did the man seem so familiar? Why couldn't he stay, and where was he going?

What a strange day it had been, beginning with Stephen showing up and calling Robert's mother "Grandma." Then all that talk about the fuzzy waves . . . Suddenly, Robert remembered a sentence from the article he'd just finished reading. It said, "Traveling through time could easily become reality within the next thirty years . . ."

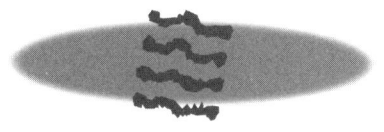

About the Illustrators

The Story Illustrator
Shaun Tan

Shaun Tan is an archaeological artist from the future, who was recently stranded in the late twentieth century, due to a technical malfunction. Since the technology required to repair his time suit won't be developed for another four centuries, Shaun is learning to live and work in the primitive world of his ancestors.

The Cover Illustrator
Marc McBride

Marc McBride has illustrated covers for several magazines and children's books. Marc currently creates the realistic images for his covers using acrylic ink with an airbrush. To solve his messy studio problem, he plans to use computer graphics instead.